E DRIVES: Overcoming Adversity

.y sales special discounts are available on quantity purchases by
.tions, associations, and others. For details, contact the publisher at the
.above.

.y U.S. trade bookstores and wholesalers. Email info@
.ublishing.net

.nd Publishing Speakers Bureau can bring authors to your live event.
.e information or to book an event contact the Beyond Publishing
. Bureau speak@BeyondPublishing.net

.or can be reached directly at BeyondPublishing.net

.ured and printed in the United States of America distributed globally
.dPublishing.net

| Los Angeles | London | Sydney

.cover: 978-1-637920-49-7

HOP

DRIVE

Overcoming Adve

Developing Resiliency And T

ELIZABETH ANN MA

BEYON
PUBLISHING

New Yor

ISBN Ha

This book is dedicated to:

Reymunda Maldonado
You have always had a passion for helping
others improve their quality of life.

TABLE OF CONTENTS

INTRODUCTION

I live on the west side of San Antonio, Texas on a street named Hope Drive. Our street curves around like a crescent shaped moon. It is my fertile crescent where I can plant seeds of hope and create a harvest of victory. Both the top and bottom part of Hope Drive have significant forks in the road. I think they symbolize the various different directions we can take in life. Each decision we make comes with its various consequences.

The bottom half of the street has a stop sign that is constantly being knocked down. It doesn't stay up for long. They replace it all the time. It ends up on the concrete in no time flat. I think it symbolizes the endless realm of possibilities that exist for each and every one of us. There is never a hard stop. There is always a continuous opportunity for growth, redefining oneself, recreating our space, and resurrecting our dreams and desires.

This is the first of a series of books named Hope Drives. My goal is to bring about awareness, create a determination to overcome adversity, and to both inspire and motivate others. This poem, by Emily Dickenson, truly illustrates just how Hope Drives.

"Hope" is the thing with feathers

By: Emily Dickinson

"Hope" is the thing with feathers-
That perches in the soul-
And sings the tune without the words-
And never stops-at all-

And sweetest in the Gale – is heard-
And sore must be the storm-
That could abash the little Bird
That kept so many warm-

I've heard in the chilliest land-
And on the strangest Sea-
Yet-never-in Extremity,
It asked a crumb-of me.

I am forty-seven years old and I have a sense of urgency to do big things. I guess I have always had the desire deep within me, but I just never pursued the actions necessary to be able to bring things to fruition. The older I get, the less I want to stay in an employee mindset. I want to venture outside of the mainstream and do something completely of my own. I encounter the naysayers, and I let their opinions cause me to talk myself out of my plans and desires for the future.

The older I get though, the tougher things seem to be. I begin to feel a deeper desire for something very different. I made the decision to go after my dreams and venture far beyond the ordinary. I want to create something that results from thinking outside the box. This creation will allow me to grow personally and professionally. I always desired to have a role in leadership, but I was never afforded the opportunity. This venture will allow me to appoint myself to this type of position.

I left my position as a certified special education teacher at the public school and began my own homeschooling program for at risk youth. People thought I had lost my mind. They said it would never take off and that I was wasting my time and talents. I ignored the naysayers and decided that the actions I take are for me and only me. The desires and dreams I have are specific to me; therefore, I do not need to seek the approval or affirmation of others in order to move forward on my quest. I am enough. I have what it takes and I pray for God's favor. I stepped out and I walked by faith and not by sight. Every day is a new beginning. It allows for me to work harder and dive deeper into my purpose. Accountability and reflection allow me to reassess and make changes to my plan of action. I can always change my plan of action, but I must stay laser focused on the goal.

I started Innovative Approaches to Education with the intention of reaching the students that fall through the cracks. Our public schools try their very best to reach everyone, but some people just need another alternative. The program has allowed me to build on my skills and talents. It has also afforded me the opportunity to improve people's quality of life. It's created and nurtured a group of life-long learners who continuously strive for more. Getting people to graduate high school is one thing, but getting people to become life-long learners is something completely different. It requires creating intrinsic motivation, growing a sense of momentum, and having the student believe they have what it takes to move to the next level. This happens after you gain their trust and they believe you have their best interest in mind. They allow themselves to be vulnerable and then give it their very best attempt to succeed. When they see they can take ownership of their own learning, and that they are making strides, they want to continue moving to the next level and they inspire others to do the same.

The homeschooling venture went even further as I saw a need for a continuum of services. People needed more one to one assistance breaking plateaus and problem solving in order to overcome obstacles. I decided to become a Life Coach. It allows me to create stronger bonds with people in my community. People are often afraid to reach out to others for help. They are afraid that people will pass judgment. They feel like they are a failure if they reach out and can't do it on their own. They couldn't be more wrong. Working together with others in order to advance is a crucial part of the learning process. The gratitude people express afterwards is unreal. So many people have been waiting for years for someone to be able to guide and encourage them. When they find success they share their experiences with others. They do it with such sincerity that the intended referral becomes another definite enrollment. Almost all of my referrals are from word of mouth. I no longer need to spend large amounts of money on advertising.

My purpose in writing this book is to inspire you to go after your dreams, your hopes, and your desires. I want you to use your God given gifts, talents, and potential to the best of your ability. Everything you need is right there within you. It is just a matter of learning how to use it. You need to pour into yourself so that you can increase your competence. You need to surround yourself with a great network of people who serve to encourage, inspire, and support your efforts. Just take the actions necessary to make your goals attainable and center yourself on your higher power. Success is a consequence of serving God.

PART 1

Who You Are And Where You Want To Go

I've always admired the Native American culture. They express pride in their culture through their dance, art, beliefs, and their sense of community. I look at their detailed works of art and quickly realize the work that went into making that artifact. I love to listen to their music and become enveloped in the emotion that it evokes. There is so much to admire in all of their works of art. Their garments display vibrant colors and detailed designs. They are amazing expressions of who they are. I attended a Pow Wow and was just amazed at the amazing ways they taught people about their culture. Native Americans have suffered many losses, but they continue to exist as one cohesive unit who stands for what they believe in and preserve their sense of morality. They do not necessarily seek to assimilate. They take pride in their authentic sense of self.

We have all had our own trials and tribulations. Some have taught us lessons and some have left lasting scars that breed wisdom and understanding. We all have our own personal Trail of Tears so to speak. We tend to leave behind a piece of ourselves in places where we feel we have been broken in spirit. Our peace sometimes is mangled into anxiety and worry. Our dreams die as we are removed from our soulful place of being. Our sanctuary of a home can become a strange and scary place when you lack peace and tranquility in your heart and mind.

If we are to reach our desired destination, we need to have a solid sense of who we are and we need to stay cemented in our beliefs, our values, and our morals. Just like athletes become experts at what they do, we need to become experts at knowing who we are and how we will react to certain situations. Athletes rely on muscle memory. They repeat the same set of actions until it becomes second nature. Our reactions to situations need to be the same way. We need to practice dealing with adversity so that we can create viable coping skills. It is not necessarily about the circumstances we are faced with. It is more about how we react to those circumstances. That is what will make us or break us.

There are so many people in the world who have untapped potential. They have God given gifts and talents that remain with them until the day they die. I urge people to explore their God given gifts and talents and to put them to use in a way that serves them and their God. There's a scripture in the bible that states, "For everyone to whom much is given, much will be required" Luke 12:48 You were called to do great things. Many people hold back because they lack the self confidence. They have a fear of failure, a lack of resources, and lack a network of people to encourage, inspire, and support them in their efforts. I encourage you to pursue your dreams and to not let fear and doubt keep you from moving forward. Believe in yourself and pray for God to put people in your path who will help you to move to that next level.

Believing in yourself and staying focused on your goal is of upmost importance. Disregard the naysayers. They will always be there. There is a bible verse in Jeremiah 29:11 that states, "For I know the plans I have for you declares the Lord, Plans to prosper you and not to harm you, Plans to give you hope and a future." There is nothing too big or too hard for God to handle. Tell yourself, "I can do all things through Christ who strengthens me." Philippians 4:13 and "If God be for us, who can be against us?" Romans 8:31 Tell yourself to "Be strong and courageous." Joshua 1:9 Go after what you want and do not let anything get in your way.

I want so much more out of life and I have a drive for making things happen. I just need the mentoring and guidance along the way. I often pave my own path rather than follow one that has been left behind. I have always been kind of an introvert, but I am willing to step outside my comfort zone to make things happen. I want to be a best-selling author, a motivational speaker, and an effective life coach. I listen to Oprah Winfrey and think that I want to be able to evoke emotion in my audience the way that she does. I want to be confident and effective as a Life Coach the way that Tony Robbins is. I want to be just like him when it comes to helping others work past road blocks and move to the next level. I admire certain aspects of the great people who are already doing what I want to do. They inspire me to keep trying and to do more.

My Life Coach certification was another tool to add to my toolbox. Although this was new to me, I hit the ground running. I started meeting with people and just being my authentic self. I could relate to the issues they were facing and my clients and I had many things in common. I know I needed to perfect my craft. There is a science to do this because there are proven techniques and strategies that work. There is also an art to it too. I needed to be able to be on the same wavelength with my clients. I needed to understand how to connect with them and how to create a hook, then give them the meat and potatoes (the content) and then be able to wrap it all up with being able to assess and evaluate our efforts.

I sought out a life coach of my own. I took part in a weekend retreat about mindset and how it affects our probability at achieving success. It was called Evolution Weekend and Daniel Gomez was our presenter. I was so glad that I attended those three days of instruction. God spoke to me through Daniel. He reassured me that I had what it took to make it big. That I needed to stop playing small time and start playing big time. I needed the guidance and inspiration that these sessions provided. It helped me lose the frustration I felt. It also taught me to change my mindset and be more intentional about moving forward. I took what I learned and I immediately put it into practice. I needed to use it or lose it.

I learned about the power of intention and I began to look at beautiful homes and expensive cars and so forth. I began to DREAM BIG and with great detail. I wanted to have a clear concrete picture at what I was aiming to attain. I began putting together a vision board. I started to write journal entries and make positive affirmations. I began to believe that all the things on my board were possible. I began to believe I was worthy. I began to believe that I could attain it and all I needed to do was to take the actions necessary to bring it to fruition.

CHAPTER ONE

Resiliency

This life is so fast paced and unpredictable. We have to be ready to react in ways that serve us. We all need to exercise our resiliency. It is our ability to bounce back after we have faced adversity or trauma. Resiliency is all about coping skills and learned responses that develop over time. I think part of it is nature and part of it is nurture. Life has a way of bringing us to our knees sometimes. Adversity or trauma affects all the different parts of wellness. It can affect our mind, our body, and even our soul. It is how we react and what we do with this adversity that makes all the difference in the world. The following quote sums up the need for resiliency. "The roads we travel in our lives often take us down a path of adversity, but if we learn from the struggle, we gain wisdom to overcome obstacles in our future." Willie Ng, MPA

Donald Meichenbaum, Ph.D. Research Director at the Melissa Institute in Miami, Florida states that 30% of the people exposed to a specific trauma or adversity will experience negative effects related to the trauma or adversity they faced. He states, "the ceiling for harmful effects is about 30% of those exposed." (Meichebaum, 2011) Individuals who are low in resilience are at risk for experiencing stress, depression, anxiety and interpersonal difficulties. (Meichebaum, 2011)

There have been times in my life where I just had no energy left in me to want to go on. I know I can really get emotionally involved in a circumstance and that it takes me a long time to be able to move forward. I tend to perseverate repeatedly replaying the series of events in my mind. I think part of it is my stubbornness and part of it is my emotions become crushed. It takes me a while to work past all of that.

Resilience allows us to maintain a healthy mindset. It allows us to be slow too anger and to be better able to problem solve. My goal in this chapter is to break resiliency down into its multiple domains so that we can understand it better. The more resilient we are the better able we will be to have healthy meaningful relationships. We will have less stress, anxiety, depression and interpersonal difficulties. We will also be able to model resilience for our younger generation so that they too may learn the same coping skills and mechanisms.

One of the domains of resiliency is reasoning. It involves the ability to problem solve, be resourceful, and to be able to anticipate and plan. We need to be able to remain open minded. We need to consider the various points of view about the specific topic too. We need to let others assist us and not undermine another person's ability to make a difference. Always keep in mind that there may be different ways to accomplish your specific goal. Sometimes we have to pivot and find another path to reach our destination.

When I think of resiliency, I think of my father, Raul Maldonado. My father was a great example of resiliency, tenacity, and perseverance. He lived through a great deal of adversity. He was born in Harlingen, Texas and grew up in Pearsall, Texas. His father walked out on his mother when he was very young. A short time later, his mother would become terminally ill. Out of sheer desperation, she would place my father and my uncle Joe (Jose Maldonado) into an orphanage. They would later be adopted by a Canadian man.

My mom and dad met at Pearsall High School. She said he was always falling asleep in class because he worked long hours at a tire shop. This was before all of the technology was in place. He did not use a machine to change the tires. He had to use a sledge hammer. In Spanish, we call it a "mazo." My mom said he was the rugged guy who worked extremely hard and that is why my grandparents loved him so much. My grandparents treated him like a son because he earned their trust and admiration. They would tell my mom that they wanted for him to be able to advance quickly because they saw his potential.

When Preparation Met Opportunity…

Their wish went straight from their mouths to God's ears. He was drafted into the military during his senior year in High School. He served in the Vietnam War. Mom said it was the best thing that could have happened to him. He excelled during his time in the military and it provided him with the structure and support he needed to be able to advance in his career. It is just a testimony to the fact that success occurs when preparation meets opportunity. I heard it said that one touch of God's favor is more than a lifetime of labor. The saying proved to be true. God has a specific plan for each and every one of us.

Dad earned the rank of Sergeant, and he successfully completed his program as an Airborne Ranger. His army days would teach him so many valuable lessons. He would endure so many defining moments. He would later use those moments to stretch my learning and it would come across in short phrases like, "How bad do you want it?", "You must not want it bad enough!" or his favorite "Lead, follow, or get out of the way!" I could go on forever about his many phrases. He used them to stimulate motivation and light a fire under my behind. He wanted me to do something to make things happen and to quit making the multiple excuses I was giving him. He would often use reverse psychology with me. He would say, "Nah, you won't do that." or "Nomas dices y no lo haces." (You just say it but you don't do it) His favorite was the deadline comment, "Cuando?"(When?) He would remind me that I was "killing daylight" and that time was of the essence.

I remember that I used to hate to hear him say those things and think damn he is so hard on me. I am grateful now for those moments. We are all grown up now, but I would not be where I am today had he not been the one to make sure we were doing what we needed to do and not getting off track. I was often pretty insecure and he always gave me the reassurance I needed to go after what it was I wanted. Sometimes, I just needed that push in the right direction.

I know life now is much more fast-paced than it was then, yet all those lessons still hold true today. He believed in being extremely intentional. He would say that you can't get somewhere without knowing how to get there. That was his way of telling me I needed to do some goal setting. I needed to have a clear plan of action for reaching my desired destination. He used to say that if you didn't let people, and circumstances, break your spirit you could do anything you set out to do. He said family had to stick together no matter what. That all we had was each other and that once he and mom were gone, it would be up to us to help each other persevere.

I think he was an excellent father. He was strict as could be though. I think he understood the need for having a supportive family atmosphere and that's why he worked so hard to maintain one. I always thought that I would marry someone who was a lot like my dad. They broke the mold though. I am still in search of that special someone who is like him. When I find them, I will reminisce and be forever thankful.

Tenacity is another one of the domains of resiliency. It involves persistence, realistic optimism, and the ability to bounce back. This requires us to have a healthy amount of self-esteem and self worth. It involves being in gratitude for what we already have. It involves thanking God for the way he has moved in our lives to bless us. Our mindset is the key to being able to overcome overwhelming obstacles and breaking through plateaus. We need to learn how to pour into ourselves and others. We can do this through self affirmations. We can begin with the end in mind. We can make vision boards and use audio recordings to enhance our senses. We need to believe that we can attain the goal. Often, people imagine that the goal has already been attained and they complete journal entries where they thank God for having blessed them with their desired outcome. We are a lot like computers in that we can program and reprogram our mindset. We are, in essence, changing our software. We can begin by saying things like: "I am able to…" or "I am worthy of…" We can state our intentions as, "I can…" or "I will…"

When dad left the military, and made his transition into civilian life, he had to redefine himself. This required him to pivot and begin his quest for stability, structure, and security. Mom and dad always had a strong sense of centeredness and focus in their higher power. They may not have been at church every given Sunday, but they had a strong spiritual sense of who they were in Christ. They understood that when they put God first in their lives, and served him, things would eventually fall into place. Dad would serve God and know that he would later reap what he now sowed. I have adopted that same principle, and it has worked for me as well.

The concept reminds me of sunflowers that face the sun to gain energy. When there is no sun they turn to face each other to give energy to one another. We too face the son SON not SUN, and we gain energy and wisdom from him that we can then pour into others by giving them information, time, compassion, and comfort. It is important that we learn how to replenish ourselves with positive energy. When we pour into others there is a transfer of energy that happens and that energy needs to be replenished so that we can still do for ourselves.

When you are down and out, you rely on your higher power to guide you and protect you. Many soldiers did not make it back from Viet Nam alive and that devastated him. Dad had many photos of people who he grew very fond of and who had died during the war. The photos have personal information about the person written on the back. When he contemplated why he was still around, he used to say, "I guess it just wasn't my time yet." I believe dad would look for the lesson in all of his personal trials. He said that going through tough times helps us to appreciate what we have and we learn not to take things for granted. He also said that we needed to learn to forgive ourselves in order to move forward in life. We all make mistakes and we learn from them. The lessons that come from the school of hard knocks are not easily forgotten. Getting through the hard times really does define our character and our beliefs.

I heard Daniel Gomez, a life coach, author, and motivational speaker, share a great analogy about the caterpillar that becomes a butterfly. He said that the caterpillar was not something that anyone really admired. They are kind of ugly creatures that crawl on the ground. Then he said, "What does the caterpillar have to do to become a butterfly?" He said they enter into the cocoon. They are by themselves. It is dark. The place is tight, and it takes time. The process does not happen right away. The butterfly has to remain in there to soak up all the nutrients. It has to gain its strength from breaking out of the cocoon because if it breaks out too soon it will die. You can't help it either. It needs to do it on its own.

We are just like the caterpillar. We often need to be by ourselves and away from all the people, all the noise, the judgments, and the crazy schedules of things to do and places to go. We need to be able to pour into ourselves and allow the Holy Spirit to do its work in us. Then, when the time is right, we can spread our wings and fly. We aren't made to crawl on the ground. "You were born to fly," as Daniel Gomez states in the title of one of his first best-selling books. We need not to settle for mediocre because we can attain so much more. Staying the course and taking action will get us to our desired destination.

We Are Constantly Evolving….

Dad had a hard time finding employment. He would interview at many places and get passed up time and time again. He wasn't waiting around though. He worked stocking merchandise, selling snow cones, and many other jobs that were not forever jobs. Then, he was finally hired at Fort Sam Houston as a mechanic, working in the motor pool. Dad earned an Associate of Applied Science from

St. Philip's in the Automotive Technology and Air Conditioning and Refrigeration fields. He loved to work with his hands and had a great combination of academic ability and technical knowledge. He was what people called a "Jack Of All Trades." He would often help people with various projects. He knew about plumbing, automotive work, and carpentry, and would even delve into the electrical field as well.

My brother, Raul, learned a lot from my dad. The two of them shared a special bond. I remember my dad taking my brother with him to go work on cars. He would carry his tools in an army green bag that looked like a miniature duffle bag. It had these two straps and a zipper that went down the middle. When Raul was too little to carry the heavy bag, he would just let him hold the handle and dad would hold the other and make him feel like he needed his help to get it from point A to point B. He was instilling the idea of working together cooperatively.

Raul would hand him tools and assist him in any way he possibly could. Dad was a lot like I am when I am under pressure. He would become a dictator. He often got stern, loud, impatient, and did not want to hear excuses. You just had to shut up and do what he said and you dare not question him when he was in the zone. He just wanted to make sure things got done and that the task was accomplished. Sometimes, that meant you had to step out of your comfort zone. Sometimes it meant working harder, faster, or just plain giving it 110% even if the task seemed impossible.

Raul recalls so many times where dad's ingenuity got them through some problem solving dilemma. They would later look back and laugh about it. After it was all over they would say, "I don't know how the hell we did that." When it came to helping us to problem solve, it was almost always done at the dinner table. Dealing with rejection, adversity, and unexpected circumstances were coping skills and learned behaviors.

Life often throws us an unexpected curveball. These are definitely moments that define us. They demonstrate who we are at our very core. They show what we believe in and where our boundaries lie. He would always tell us to stay true to who we were. He said you have to stand for what you believe in because that is what makes great leaders. Otherwise, you are just a follower and you will never grow.

Another important domain of resiliency is composure. It is all about being able to regulate emotions. It involves the ability to see the bias in interpreting the circumstances, and the ability to remain calm and in control.

Dad understood the need for having a balance of routine and novelty. Dad was a short man, stout, and wide shouldered. He lived his life constantly working and always on the go. He was very much a family man though. I remember we would take long drives on the weekends with no real destination in mind. We would always end up out in the country somewhere. He would look at old structures, or remnants of what once was, and say there's a lot of history there. I think it was nostalgic for him because it would bring him back to his roots and memories of his childhood. He would often talk about moving to the country. I think his soul craved that red dirt and those wide open fields.

I also remember that when we were growing up we always had a bunch of kids at the house. We always showed a great deal of hospitality and enjoyed people's company. One of dad's great past times was to watch movies with us in the living room. We would open up the sleeping bag and spread it on the floor. We would put a big bowl of popcorn in the middle so that we could share. He loved spending time at Blockbuster Video looking for his favorite types of movies. He loved the action flicks and I loved the dramas and documentaries. He would say I was a nerd. I liked the sad stuff or the stuff that had to do with studying a certain concept.

Dad had a love for Jazz and Blues Music. I have always enjoyed it too. It had a way of capturing our attention and taking our emotions to another place. I know he loved BB King because he had a way of playing the guitar and singing about love and solitude. The lyrics created a common ground that others could relate to. It created a balance of routine and novelty to take time out to enjoy the music. It was always accompanied by great food and drinks. The experience was something to really enjoy because it did not happen often enough.

A good balance of routine and novelty brings about a healthy sense of composure. Giving ourselves time to take in the information, and data we have collected, and letting it sink in is important. Too many times, we tend to make decisions when we are emotional and that does not result in good decision making. I always say we have to let it marinate. When you cook meat and you let it marinate it is much softer and not so tough. Life itself is easier to chew when you let it marinate and we aren't so quick to react.

Vision is another important part of resiliency. Vision requires us to examine our purpose. It deliniates our goals, and it requires for our goals, and for our practices to be in congruence with those goals and objectives. Part of having vision is asking ourselves questions like "What is my why?" In business, we write down our mission statement. When we write goals, we need to ask ourselves if the goals are SMART goals. Are they Specific? Are they Measureable? Are they Attainable? Are they Realistic? Are they Timely? We need to have both long term and short term goals. We need to have objectives and a plan of action for how we are going to attain these goals. We need to ask ourselves if our objectives and plan of action is congruent with reaching our goals. Are they in line with our vision? Does it fit what we are trying to do?

Dad had a lot of vision. He would have certain things he wanted to do and he would tell us just how he was going to make it happen. In a way it was like he had us to hold him accountable. He would often check back with us and say ok I am closer to meeting the goal. Sometimes, he would say well it is going to take me longer than I thought. Either way, he was teaching us how to have vision and how to go about goal setting and putting a plan of action into practice.

He often said that vision was totally about a person's perspective. It did not have to match anyone else's vision. It was totally your own. His vision for his family was pretty solid. It was unique in that he made it malleable. As we grew older, he would tell us what he wanted for us. It changed from time to time to meet the needs of the family and society in general. I liked that he was not stuck in the societal roles of man and woman. He enjoyed cooking Sunday breakfasts in the kitchen with mom. He was a great cook too. I remember when mom had gall bladder surgery and had to be admitted to the hospital. He took on her role at home. My brother Raul and I were thinking "Oh My God! Let's see how this is going to turn out." Dad had big shoes to fill. Mom did a lot at home. She cooked, cleaned, washed, nurtured etc… We were shocked when he busted out with four course meals that included handmade desserts. He made a chocolate cake in a cast iron skillet one day. It was to die for! I had not seen that part of dad before and it made me really appreciate the bond that he and mom shared. It was definitely special and out of the ordinary.

I admired the way that they worked together to give us what we needed. Dad worked super hard to make the money and mom was a great caregiver not just to us but to grandma and grandpa too. My grandmother had to undergo dialysis treatments and there were so many times when she felt super weak. She was often so ill she needed assistance getting out of bed, getting dressed and other basic tasks. Mom helped her every step of the way. My grandfather developed stomach cancer years after my grandmother had died. He required help with all his basic living skills. We learned to use a Hoyer, transfer him from the bed to the wheel chair, changing him, dressing him, etc… I thank God for the blessing of having been brought up in a home where I had both my parents and both my grandparents to help nurture me. They were committed and they endured many hardships to provide what I needed. I know I remember reciting my dad's eulogy and saying that we may not have had luxuries, but we had the love of a father. That, to me, was more valuable than all the luxuries of the world. I remember feeling that deep in my soul.

The last domain in resiliency has to do with health. This involves getting enough sleep at night. The idea is to be able to get at least six to eight hours of uninterrupted sleep each night. Eating right and exercising are key components as well. This was definitely the domain where we all were lacking. We grew up with the traditional hispanic culture of eating unhealthy food. I remember mom and grandma would cook using the Crisco can and a large serving spoon. They would scoop out the Crisco shortening with a large metal spoon and then put the shortening in the pan they were cooking in. Of course no one complained because the food was always delicious. Unfortunately, we would all become diabetics. I know genetics played a large role too.

The idea of eating healthy is so important. I know diabetics tend to have high blood pressure and high cholesterol and then inevitable kidney failure. It is a combination of illness and disease that is both costly to treat and uncomfortable to deal with. If I ever raise a family of my own, I will keep this domain at the top of the list. It is so important. We don't realize just how important it is until we are faced with the negative consequences of not making it a priority.

I urge you to revisit these five domains of resiliency. They help us to stay healthy and make us better able to deal with life in general. I know it is not easy. I have heard people say, "Yard by yard is hard, but inch by inch is a cinch." The phrase holds very true. Start to work on one domain and master it. Then go on to work on the other domains so that you will eventually be able to improve your quality of life in a way that best serves you and your loved ones.

Chapter Summary/Key Takeaways

- Resiliency encompasses: vision, composure, reasoning, health, and tenacity

- Vision includes purpose, goals, and congruence

- Composure includes: regulating emotions, identifying interpretation bias, and being calm and in control

- Reasoning includes: problem solving, resourcefulness, and being able to anticipate and plan

- Health includes: nutrition, sleep, and exercise

- Tenacity includes: persistence, realistic optimism, and being able to bounce back

- Take time to write out your goals. Create a precise vision about what you want in life. Create a journal entry about it. State specifically how you want it to be.

- In the next chapter, you will learn about Dreaming Big

CHAPTER TWO

Dreaming Big

I love spending time outdoors. There is such a peace about being outside and being at one with nature. I especially enjoy the sound of running water. It is so soothing. I love the cool breeze and the feeling of the sun on my skin. I know I don't get to spend too many moments being fully present in those types of environments because I am always trying to run around keeping up with everything. My desire is to be able to be truly present in the moment. I want to have the ability to truly soak in the spirit of all the living things around me. I am very sensitive to my surroundings and I enjoy the colors, the smells, and the feelings I get from being in specific environments. Just soaking my feet in the water and feeling the sand between my toes makes me happy. I think that people can sense such a deeper connection to others, and to the universe, when we are not overwhelmed with all the multiple things there is to do and places to go.

This is what inspires me to dream big. I want to be financially stable enough to be able to periodically remove myself from my work. I want to enjoy the world by being totally present during the special moments. Making it big would allow me to enjoy myself and others in such a more impactful way. Money would be more abundant. Although money does not bring us happiness, it is a resource that makes life a lot easier. I have seen just how much easier it is when you have more money. If I can make things easier for myself, and those I love, then I definitely want to do that.

Dreaming big is essential if we are to be successful in our life project. As children, we are not afraid to dream big. As we grow older though, we tend to stick to the small stuff and are afraid to try for things that we think are out of reach or more difficult to attain. We tend to think that we are limited to our current condition, but that is clearly not the case at all. If you have a passion for achieving a specific goal, then you are going to do everything in your power to make it happen. We need to take time to rekindle our own flame. We all have passions for certain things in life and somehow we let our experiences and our negative self talk influence us into blowing out the flame.

We express limiting beliefs when we say, "That will never happen for me." The enemy wants us to give up because there is such a power and profound presence in us that it threatens the evil works that lurk among us here on Earth. The enemy exists to be able to lie, cheat, kill, and destroy. It robs us of our joy and our energy. We need to replace the negative self talk with positive self talk saying, "I am more than a conqueror." You can say things like, "I am the head and not the tail." There is always ways to replace the negative behaviors with the positive ones. It is all part of having a change of mindset.

We need to walk by faith and not by sight. God will open doors you thought would never be opened. We need to think and say, "I can do all things through Christ who strengthens me." He will make all things possible. It is our intentions and our mindset that either allow us to grow or block our ability to move forward in life.

I know I had limiting beliefs I had to let go. I thought you had to have money to make money. I thought that I had to hold on to the money because there was not much of it to go around. That limiting mindset is what kept me from moving forward.

I remember attending a workshop where they had us do some free writing. The prompt was about being a millionaire. We were to say what we would do as a millionaire that we couldn't do otherwise. It really opened up the realm of possibilities for me. I had never really thought about being a millionaire. It just never crossed my mind. I think that limited my beliefs. I was blocking that from happening to me by telling the universe that I did not will that it into existence. Later on, I thought why couldn't that happen for me? Why wouldn't it? I serve the God of the great multitude. There is more than enough to go around. I just needed to go get mine. I left the seminar feeling so excited that I really couldn't sleep well that night.

Believing in Myself

I realized that the realm of possibilities in my life depended solely on my belief in myself and my mindset. I needed to dream big if I was going to want to make it big. The human spirit relies on so much of what we are conditioned to believe. There is definitely a need for us to change our programming. We need to tell ourselves that we are enough. That we have what it takes to make it big in life. Tell yourself that the world is out there for us to grab a hold of and enjoy. Self affirmations are a great way to do this type of thing. Journaling as if you have already attained the desired goal is just another way to help you reprogram your mind. Vision boards and other visuals are also great ways to stimulate a positive mindset.

Dreaming Big opens the door to greater possibilities in life. If you go to the same places all the time, it gets boring. Life is the same way. Venture out and strive for the big stuff. There's a saying that says if you shoot for the moon and you don't make it at least you will end up among the stars. It is so true. We can move to the next level when we put our focus on that task. When we go all in we can accomplish just about anything we set out to do.

Constantly Reassess Your Circle of Influence

I had to remove myself from the naysayers. I had to reassess my group of people that I spent my time with. When I took time to tell them about great things that happened to me, they did not respond with the sense of enthusiasm and joy I expected from them. I also noticed that they were constantly criticizing and making comments about how they thought I was dreaming too much. They thought I did not have it in me to do the things I had set out to do. It was very disappointing. I realized that I would leave their place and feel depleted of my energy and my spirit was not at peace anymore.

We are all influencers. We can influence others and we can influence ourselves in various ways. I was allowing others to influence me to give up on my dreams. I was allowing them to influence me to think I wouldn't make it. It was making me feel like I was less than who God created me to be.

When I changed the group of people that I spent most of my time with, I was able to continue to dream big. It was like I had opened up a door that had remained closed for a long time. I realized I had been cheating myself out of so many opportunities for advancement. I had to make up for lost time! I began going to seminars. I began to read books. I watched inspirational videos of people who had gone from rags to riches. I enjoyed life so much more when I removed myself from the naysayers. I was very surprised to see just how much my self esteem improved once I did.

I have always been the type of person who roots for the underdog. I always saw it as a challenge to take a person who was at an all time low and boost them up to where they felt empowered. I enjoyed seeing the transformation. It was self-fulfilling for me to know that I had a part in it. As individuals, I think we need to learn how to do that for ourselves. I needed to feel inspired. I needed to feel empowered, and mostly I needed to feel confident. I had to explore the various ways in which I could change my vibration. The vibration we put out into the universe has a predetermined response.

Life has so many different variables. We need to know how to manipulate the variables so that they become catalysts for success. Habits either help or hinder our success. Habits are simply repeated actions that we take without even thinking about it. I started replacing my bad habits with good ones so that I could have a better chance at success. If I am going to dream big I want to increase my chances at reaching my desired destination.

Once I felt more confident and secure, I began to dream big and really go after what I wanted. We have to make sure the conditions are right so that we can prosper. We are not like weeds that just grow anywhere. We need the conditions to be just right. When we are given the proper care and nurturing, we are able to advance.

Chapter Summary/Key Takeaways

- Dreaming big requires special conditions

- Believe in yourself

- Remove the naysayers

- Constantly reassess your circle of influence

- Constantly create favorable conditions

- Increase your self esteem

- Focus on your goals

- Stay committed

- Write down three big dreams that you want to accomplish

- Write out ways to create favorable conditions for reaching these big dreams.

- In the next chapter, you will learn about being intentional.

PART II

Getting To Your Desired Destination

Getting to our desired destination requires a multifaceted approach: a clear cut plan of action that includes goals and objectives, believing in yourself, and staying the course. The hardest part of getting to your destination is the beginning. Get started. Take the first steps, and then just keep going. Once you gain momentum it is easier to keep going. It becomes difficult when you stop and then want to start again. Begin with the end in mind. Know that every step you take is getting you closer to your desired destination. Sometimes we take baby steps and sometimes we take giant leaps. The point is to keep moving forward. Do not rely on others for affirmation. Believe in yourself and remain focused. There will always be skeptics.

Our Stories Deserve To Be Told

Everyone has a story to tell. Sharing our story and making our mark makes a difference. I plan to be able to share my story with the world and have them relate to the ups and the downs. I think that people seek assistance from those that they can relate to and with those they find a common ground. I know I tend to want to be with people who are just like I am. There is a comfort in knowing that they can relate to my circumstance and my current situation.

We will all make mistakes and we will learn from them. Welcome the mishaps because they will be part of the growing process. I know we all avoid failure and chaos but sometimes when we are faced with that we learn more profoundly. It is not every day that we learn from the school of hard knocks. When we do, it isn't easily forgotten.

My goal is to help people be proactive in their efforts and intentional in their actions. I have helped many people improve their quality of life, but I could not do it without their desire for change. They had to want it. I had to want it too. I had to have the desire for change. I want to be able to look back and laugh at the crazy things that happened. I want to look back and think I remember when I failed at this or that, but look where I am now. It is all possible if we want it bad enough. If we keep striving for what we desire we will eventually get there. I know I learn best when things are predictable and consistent. I learn best when I have frequent feedback. When I know what is expected of me, who I can go to for help, and I get feedback about my progress, then I know I can make it. It just means I have to have the right conditions in place. Everybody has different needs and I make it my job to see what those needs are and to help them have those needs met. At times it requires being a point of contact for people and giving them the information they need in order to get the right services.

Building An Empire

I want to build an empire! I want it to be a solid foundation that I can add to as time goes on. I want it to attract people because it has real results that people can access anytime and anywhere. Our world has become so automated and technological. I want to embrace that and use those features to help reach people and service them. I would love to build a solid clientele that grows steadily. I am dreaming big and giving my dreams a concrete sense of being. I am writing my dreams and desires down. I imagine what my dream house will look like. I saw a house I loved online. It was $19,750,000! I printed it out and saved the video they had of the inside of the place. I play it over and over and imagine myself owning a place like that. I also printed a picture of a Ferrari. Why not? If I can dream why not go for it! It gave me inspiration to work harder and strive for more. Let those who criticize say what they may. I love the idea of being able to work and make something of myself. I love the idea of learning all I can. I developed a love of learning early in life and I knew it would serve me later in life. If I am coachable, and I try my best to attain the goals I have in mind. Why wouldn't I be successful? I know I can do it. I just need to put my behind in gear. I need to go into overdrive. I have been stuck in slow and stop and that just is not working for me anymore. I desire to have more. I desire to do more. I need to work hard to be able to make it happen.

I am forming a new circle of influence. I am trying my best to pour into myself and be able to move forward with God Speed. I know I need to be able to lean on those who truly want what is best for me. I know I need to surround myself with those who are currently where I want to go. I know I am a good student and that is what will allow me to grow. If we are going to be catalysts for change, we need to be selective about what we allow around us. I want to surround myself with people who are for me and not against me. People who take a vested interest in me moving forward and advancing personally and professionally. This requires me to be selective about whom I bring into my inner circle. People can either build you up or tear you down. Start to assess who is who in your life. I need people who add to me not subtract from me.

My desire is to be a motivational speaker, life coach, author, and teacher. I want to uplift and inspire others to move past their current circumstances. I want to be a part of their growth. I want to be able to see them reach places they never thought they would reach. The development will inspire others to do the same. I know people are always watching what others do. They believe in the process when they see others reach their ultimate destination.

CHAPTER THREE

Being Intentional

Being intentional is extremely important. From the time we get up in the morning, to the time we go to bed, we need to be intentional about our way of thinking and our behaviors. We have to keep a positive mindset. Our actions should always help us achieve our goals.

I had to start my day with positive affirmations and positive intentions. I needed to write them down. I needed to say them. I needed to listen to audio recordings that told me I was enough. I had to listen to audio recordings that said I had what it took to make it big. I needed to watch videos about people who went from rags to riches. It was not just inspiring, but affirming. I heard about people who went to the same schools I went to. They were very rich people. I heard about how they overcame difficult circumstances. I also realized that I needed to see myself in that same light.

The idea of moving to the next level seems hard when we think of how we have to step outside of our comfort zone. It is hard to take risks. It is hard to think that we may fail. What I did know was that it was harder for me to just give up and think that I couldn't rise above my current circumstances. I had no intention in staying stagnant and living with regrets. I did not want to think that I could have, would have, should have, but didn't. I needed to take every opportunity to advance and undoubtedly say I will.

Believing Who I Am Is Enough

I knew I had a calling. Whether other people saw it or not didn't matter. All I needed was to acknowledge I had a task to fulfill here on Earth. I needed to do it with the same passion that God had when he put that gift in me to share with the world. I needed to not let people's opinions or judgments get in my way. I needed to rise above all of that and just do me. I often hear people say, "Just do you boo!" They couldn't be more right. We worry too much about what others think or how they will react. I think stepping out in our own authority is the ultimate demonstration of faith. To have faith that God will supply, encourage, and nurture our calling is truly to live by faith and not my sight.

I need a clear plan of action. I need to write short term and long term goals with objectives that delineate a step by step process on how I will reach my goal. I pray that God will place people in my path that will assist me to get to that next level. I realized I needed to be open to the possibilities that existed in my life. I began to interact with people who were successful doing what it was I wanted to do. It inspired me to do so much more than what I was doing currently.

Know That What You Desire is Possible

The possibility that I could reach the next level seemed so much more real to me. I knew that if I took the right actions that it would eventually pay off. I just had to build the confidence and profound belief in myself and know I could get there.

I needed to GPS my future. When you GPS a location you have to input your current location and then you input the desired destination. The GPS even asks you if you want to take a shorter, faster route, or if you don't mind the scenic view. Our plans for the future should be the same way. They should map out different ways to attain the same desired result. Sometimes, we have to avoid the traffic or the light after light by going on the highway instead. Our future decisions will often have variations of attaining the same desired goal. It is good to envision one way but know that others exist in case we have to change directions. It is good to anticipate what may happen to keep us from reaching our desired destination. Planning and problem solving are both key elements in the realm of achievement and success.

I needed to see who my support system was going to be. Who was going to help me get there? Who could I go to if I needed to vent or to problem solve my way past an obstacle? It was important to know who my safety net was going to be. I needed to know who I could go to that would not pass judgment and make me feel like I was less than who God made me to be.

Once I was able to GPS my future, and figure out whom my support system was, I was ready to take the actions I needed to take. Now I was able to venture out, take risks, and step outside my comfort zone with courage and faith. I would take the necessary actions to grow my learning.

Chapter Summary/Key Takeaways

- Believe in yourself and step out in confidence.

- Surround yourself with people who are already doing what it is you want to do.

- Keep in mind that this will take time and effort and stay focused.

- Create a safety net of people who will support, encourage and inspire you.

- Create a list of ways that you can surround yourself with people who will inspire, support, and encourage you.

- What are some actions you can take that will make you become more intentional in your efforts at attaining your desired goals?

- In the next chapter, you will learn about Self Care.

CHAPTER FOUR

Self Care

Selfcare is about taking care of you before you can take care of others. Self Care is not being selfish. So many times we get caught up in being there for other people and we put ourselves last. It often makes us feel depleted. We lack the energy and the drive to do much for ourselves when we are constantly doing for others.

Take Time to Reflect

I had to set aside time for me to be alone and at one with my higher power. It did not necessarily have to require that I be in church. It did not require that I isolate myself in the wilderness either. I just needed alone time so that I could think, be inspired, and process my actions and emotions. Sometimes, it meant being on the front porch at night and taking in all that happened during the day. Breaking down the many things that occurred, helped me to realize how I could have done better. There was a sense of therapeutic rapport that was necessary. Taking time to reexamine what has happened is crucial if we are going to learn and grow.

I did not always do that type of reflecting before. I would just go on and never really reexamine like I should have. I would just get things done and move on. I call it being in survival mode. I never took time to go back and analyze and interpret data so that it made more sense. I needed to look at things from various perspectives so that I could truly understand where the other people were coming from. I needed to seek first to understand before I could be understood.

I also needed a way to be able to refill my soul. This included refilling myself emotionally, physically, and spiritually. There were various ways I could do this. I enjoy all types of music. I like being outside. I love the sound of running water. I also enjoyed spending time with other adults in a place where it was a relaxed and enjoyable atmosphere. All of these things allowed me to fill myself back up with energy, enthusiasm, and hope.

Find Your Quiet Place

I know we are not all the same, but you have to find the things you enjoy. Find things that allow you to feel relaxed. Find things that you can do that allow you to feed your spiritual sense too. I enjoy just sitting quietly in a chapel and taking in the spirit that exists there. You do not necessarily have to do anything, but be in reverence with the spiritual sense that exists in the place. I loved going to The Grotto because it was outdoors and I could simply be at peace in a quiet place where I could pray or leave flowers in gratitude for the blessings I had received. I could light candles and leave them in petition for the things I was praying about.

There is something about taking people out of their everyday environment, and allowing them to experience something new, that just feeds the soul. I love seeing the maple trees turn different colors and to watch the leaves just add color to the landscape. I also like to feel the cool breeze outside while enjoying a picnic or just eating outdoors. I prefer that instead of being inside all the time.

Finding Joy in Letting Go

Learning to say the word "no" was crucial to my sense of wellness. I tended to want to be a people pleaser. I would spread myself thin. I made it more difficult for myself to do the self care I needed. I was too busy trying to please everyone else. Often times, the gestures I made were not even appreciated. I was often taken for granted. As a matter of fact, I would notice some people would walk in and out of my life often and that the only time I would hear from them was when they needed something. I started to shy away from those types of people because I saw them as energy vampires. They would just suck the life right out of me. They only looked for me when they were in crisis. I only had myself to blame though because I would never say no. I always felt bad for them or I thought that saying no was being mean. Truth was that I needed to set healthy boundaries..

Time Is A Nonrenewable Resource

What I later realized was that time was a nonrenewable resource and that they were depleting me of it. Those were hours I would never get back. When I realized just how much time I wasted on people who had no intention of even building a real relationship with me it made me feel bad. I needed to learn to value my time. I needed to teach them to value my time too because I would agree to help them with something and set some time aside for them and they inevitably would come hours late or hours earlier causing me havoc.

Eating right and getting enough sleep is of great importance too. I often had trouble sleeping. It always seemed that just when I was able to go to bed and actually fall asleep I would get the late night phone call or text that required attention. I needed to set healthy boundaries. That in itself was a great sense of self care.

The idea of having a good balance in your life is key. Do for you. Love yourself enough to give yourself what you need to feel good. Give yourself permission to put yourself first. It is good to be centered. When you are in alignment with the universe, great things start to happen. It is when we are out of balance with the universe, that we encounter feelings of frustration. It is important to constantly assess what we are doing and if it is making us happy or not. This constant reassessment allows us to adjust our behavior and our practices to meet our needs.

Once we learn to take better care of ourselves, we will see that we can accomplish more. Peace and tranquility allow for inspiration and creativity to exist. I could never be creative or inspired when I was running like a chicken with my head cut off. I had to nurture myself with setting the right conditions in place. Self care also requires surrounding ourselves with good role models and people who will advocate or mentor us. There are people out there that are willing to share what they have learned. They are people who are willing to pay it forward.

Chapter Summary/Key Takeaways

- Time is a nonrenewable resource.

- Be aware of whom, and on what, you are spending your time.

- It is ok to say no.

- Take time out to do things that make you happy.

- Allow yourself time to reflect and evaluate.

- Write down things that you can do to make you happy and give you a good balance of me time and time with others.

- What things can you say no to that would allow you more time for yourself?

- In the next chapter, you will learn about Paying It Forward.

CHAPTER FIVE

Paying it Forward

My dad died when he was twenty-one years old. He was the stability, security, and serenity that existed in my life. He had a heart attack at home. My brother Raul and I administered CPR but we were unable to save him. My two youngest siblings Sonny (6 yoa) and Marcelina (was 11 yoa) stood in the doorway watching Raul and I try to save him. They had this awful look of fear on their faces and I remember telling my mom to take them somewhere else. Everything happened so fast and my life would be forever changed. I was twenty-two at the time and Raul was nineteen.

Surviving Heartbreak and Finding Strength

As a result of experiencing traumatic events, some individuals will experience POST TRAUMATIC GROWTH (PTG) PTG is the ability to experience positive personal changes that result from the struggle to deal with trauma and the consequences. PTG highlights that strengths can emerge through suffering and struggles with adversities. Individuals may develop a renewed appreciation for life and commitment to live life to the fullest, valuing each day; improved relationships with loved ones; a search for new possibilities and enhanced personal strengths and new spiritual changes (Meichenbaum, 2011).

I believe I experienced Post Traumatic Growth because I had a solid devotion and determination to make positive change occur. Once dad died, Raul and I did everything we could to support my mom in raising our two younger siblings Marcy and Sonny. Come to think of it, it is the closest I have ever come to being a parent. Raul, mom and I, took such pride in guiding and encouraging Marcy and Sonny.

I remember Sonny performing at an elementary talent show. He had stayed home from school that day but he decided he was still going to attend the talent show that evening. The coach, who was the Master of Ceremonies, introduced him as coming from his death bed to perform. He knocked the socks off of the other contestants with the love song that he sang. He made the crowd go wild. I cried as he took command of the stage with such confidence. He had such a love of music and enjoyed the arts. When he was in High School, he performed with the school choir. They performed "Mary Did You Know" for a Christmas concert. The performance was done in a new brick rotunda building and they stood on the stairs of a winding staircase. The acoustics there were simply amazing! Their rendition was done as a round which really showcased the various octaves in such a miraculous way. He wore a black tuxedo and looked so sharp. Those two moments in Sonny's life truly illustrated to me just how important it is to pay it forward and just how much people can attain when they are nurtured and cared for.

Marcy attended John Marshall High School. I would drive her to school in the mornings and drop her off on my way to work at the Northside Alternative Middle School-North Campus. I was a special education teacher there. I worked primarily with students who were diagnosed with a Learning Disability and/or an Emotional Disturbance. Those morning drives were always opportunities for me to set the day up for her with encouragement, inspiration, and motivation. I wanted her to walk with confidence and to know that I was approachable for anything she ever needed to discuss. That meant that I had to be real with her and I had to be willing to touch those touchy subjects that were not so easy to discuss. I needed to be careful how I worded things and I had to understand that my actions would breed specific reactions from her. I had to be ready for what she would dish out and remain the reality base in the situation. To this day, my siblings and I are very real with one another and we are pretty blunt and tell it like it is. We don't worry about being politically correct. We just know that the dialog has to happen and that it is important to keep the dialog happening.

Intentional Examples...

I remember when she was still in elementary school and I would take her with me to my summer school teacher certification classes at The University of Texas at San Antonio. She was always well behaved. She was extremely observant. We would visit the University Center and she loved being part of what went on there. I intentionally wanted to expose her to what I was doing. I wanted her to follow in my footsteps and one day earn a degree. The huge auditoriums full of people did not intimidate her. It was like second nature to her after a while. I know I had to get used to all of that. I was not used to being in class with so many people. As a matter of fact I would later learn that it did not fit my learning style. I learned best when I was in a small group. That was something I learned from the school of hard knocks too.

Marcy is now a Special Education Coordinator at a middle school campus. I am so proud of her. She has such a passion for serving others. She multitasks better than anyone I know. She is now married and has two daughters who she is extremely intentional with. She does a lot of what I call milieu management. She manages the way she sets up the area where the kids are going to do their school work. She limits the amount of items available to them in that area. There is always room for improvement and they know it. I love the open conversations she has with the girls too. I know they see her as being approachable too. She and her husband Roman have parenting styles that complement one another. Roman is the disciplinarian and Marcy is the therapeutic counselor type.

My brother, Raul, is just the way my dad was. He has such a strong sense of self-worth. He wanted to be a fire fighter and I wanted to be a police officer. Neither one of us ever was ever able to get that chance to serve that way, but I guess it was not God's plan for us. Raul completed fire school and became an EMT-Basic. I ended up switching majors from Criminal Justice to Interdisciplinary Studies and beginning my teaching career. We all chose careers in the helping professions. Raul truly has a passion for being a servant leader.

He is currently a supervisor at a company that does demolition work. He runs a crew of laborers and oversees the jobs: making sure they stay on schedule, making sure the employees' needs are being met, that the environment is safe, and making sure that the equipment they need is furnished in a timely manner. He and I talk a lot about how important it is to have a positive sense of morale. We both know that there is a direct correlation between morale and production. People perform better when you show them that they matter and that they are appreciated. He plants seeds of hope by offering the upper management techniques and strategies they can implement in order to improve morale in the workplace. Little by little he is seeing positive change. He says that things don't happen overnight and that is very true. He engages in authentic experiences so that the guys feel appreciated. He does things like making snow cones on Fridays when the Texas heat is over 100 degrees. He brings them popsicles and cold canned drinks as well. He has given them safety sunglasses to wear and he and I worked together to get the crew sunscreen, sun block and lip balm with a strong SPF. He tells me that he also encounters the naysayers too. The bottom line is that it all improves productivity, increases positive morale, and develops cohesion. I am just amazed at the way he connects with others. He is selfless and empathetic. I love that about him.

I Learned How To Really Live

So many times we go through the motions in life and we do not realize just how important everything is. I once took things for granted, but now have realized just how precious life is. Things can change in a matter of seconds. We need to truly value the blessings that God gives us. We also need to do what we can to be of service to others.

The enemy attacks us in the places where we are the most vulnerable. He looks for ways to injure and attack. Our family truly faced the worse sense of adversity when our youngest sibling became addicted to drugs. Sonny was the youngest in the family. No one in our family uses drugs. Someone outside the family would introduce him to that life. We would endure endless anxiety and strife. People do not realize the pain and agony that an addict's family endures. He would endure endless battles for his sobriety. It would kill me to see how hard we all worked to help him with his sobriety just to see him go right back to that life.

The same people who introduced him to that mess would hover around like buzzards just waiting to pull him in the other direction. It caused me such anger and frustration. We would endure so many unpredictable moments that caused us all to be in survival mode. It kills me that these same people are still operating the way they do. They are ruining so many other families.

I had a young man come tell me just recently that drug dealers are just like everyone else. That everyone has a hustle and that they have to make their money somehow. I felt my stomach cringe and I felt my face get hot. I know the person who said this is young and inexperienced, but I did say that it ruins people's lives and ruins families. I know without a shadow of a doubt that if you live in sin that you will bear the consequences of death and destruction. There are no gray areas as far as I am concerned. If you live by the sword you die by the sword. There is also no honor among thieves. These people rob people of a healthy and meaningful life. I don't preach to them because I know that people who are going to leave that life need to have an intrinsic motivation to change. They have to want it. You can give them everything, but until they are ready you will not see change. It has to be a vested interest in changing their high risk lifestyles.

I saw just how bad the neighborhood had become and I vowed to be a part of the solution. I tried my best to work with law enforcement to increase the police presence. I wanted law enforcement to work cooperatively with the immediate community. It would be a lot more complicated that I realized. People run interference for others and the whole thing is bigger than I ever imagined. All I can do is pray for our community. One thing is for sure. The life you choose to live determines your outcome. You can't prosper when you live doing things that are not of God. The consequences affect so many other people besides themselves. It affects the immediate community because it breeds crime and compromises safety.

Sonny, as many addicts do, involved himself in high risk behavior. He was hit by a car and almost died. He had to endure a long stay at the hospital, brain surgery, leg surgeries, being on a ventilator, physical rehabilitation, speech therapy, and occupational therapy. The traumatic brain injury he endured would change his ability to reason and his impulsivity was much greater that it was before. He would have to learn to walk again, and talk again. He would have to learn new ways to adapt and complete independent living skills. He had to learn to dress himself again. He had to learn a new way to shower, new ways to use the restroom, new ways to eat independently etc… I am sure you can see how I totally disagree with the thought that drug dealers need to make their money and have their hustle just like everybody else. I hate drugs and I know they only lead to death and destruction.

Unfortunately, there is no handbook for dealing with addiction. Sonny had enrolled in barber school and we all hoped for the best. We wanted him to learn a skill. No matter what we did, he needed to deal with that underlying issue before we could get him to a better place. Sonny would succumb to his addiction. He overdosed. I was crushed with such a sense of grief, guilt, anger, and desperation. My heart ached because I constantly argued with him. I wanted him to change. I wanted him to improve.

I did not have the training or tools for dealing with addiction. I still don't. I just felt lost and empty. I was angry at God for a long time. I was angry at the world and like many people who go through a tough time, I asked God, "Why?" I asked, "Why us?" "Why couldn't my family be a happy healthy family like everyone else?" "What did we do to deserve this?" The questions just kept coming. It was a rage that I could not get rid of. I was unable to function the way I would normally do. It was just so hard to move forward and continue on. I felt cheated. I felt undeserving. I felt wretched.

These experiences have given me a greater sense of empathy for families who are dealing with addiction. Now, I look for ways to assist people who may be spiraling into addiction and participating in high risk behaviors. My siblings are the same way. God has given us opportunities to work with individuals who are recovering from addiction and we are empathetic to their needs and the needs and their families. We are all looking for ways to pay it forward in a significant manner. We want to prevent this type of thing from happening to any other family. It is something that truly rocks you to your very core.

I learned to really live when I was able to find a way of letting go of the anger, the frustration, and the heartache that came from such a severe loss. It took a lot of working through my feelings, and understanding my circumstances, before I could find the energy to keep on moving forward. We all grieve in our own way, but I felt numb and stuck in the aftermath. The amount of grief consumed me. I felt like no one could really understand the way I felt because they had not been through what I had been through.

One of the happiest moments I had in serving the needs of others was when my brother Raul and I conducted a two day workshop in Crystal City with a nonprofit called (MET) Motivation Education and Training. We were working with at risk youth and helping them to earn their High School Diploma. For being our first time, it was a great success! My mom tagged along with us and it was a very positive trip. We were welcomed with open arms. MET had a vested interest in building a solid foundation for the youth. Mr.

Frailan Sendejo, the workforce development coordinator, even invited people from Eagle Pass to take part in the workshop. We had such a feeling of self satisfaction as we drove back home. We had created positive change in the lives of the many students who attended the workshop. We brought them the hope that would drive them towards a brighter future. They wanted change, so they attended. We simply sought them through the process. It is a great feeling to reach someone at just the right time when they are motivated to learn and want to continue to advance.

Rejecting the Apathy

Our neighborhood needed some work and attention too. I saw a need to be a catalyst for hope and positive change in our immediate community. I prayed to God asking him to make me an instrument of his will. I knew I would make a good servant leader because I had a passion for improving the community. I wanted the people in our immediate community to feel empowered. I wanted them to become actively involved. I wanted them to make the environment more nurturing for our youth and I wanted there to be a sense of synergy. Everything seemed so segmented and there was such a pessimistic outlook about improving the current condition of the community.

Finding The Passion

Sometimes, having a passion comes from doing something you love and sometimes passion comes from doing something about what angers you. There were two drug houses in our immediate area and they were a nuisance. Our house had also been burglarized twice before I got angry enough that I developed an undeniable passion for positive change.

I used a social platform called Next Door to be able to invite residents to my home. I asked them to take part in some Citizens on Patrol sessions that the San Antonio Police Department offered. Woodlawn Hills Neighborhood Association President Ruben Sanchez responded to my invitation. He not only reached out to take part in the gathering, but he facilitated the mission by creating necessary contacts with city, state, and county leaders. It would be the start of a very close friendship. Problem solving and communication are two things we work on regularly.

SAFFE (San Antonio Fear Free Environment) Officer Elliott Valdez came to my home to train all of the participants on how to report suspicious activity and crime in our neighborhood. I served pizza, garden salad with all the fixings, cheese cake, tea, and soft drinks because a lot of people were headed to the session immediately after they left work. I gave away door prizes too. I absolutely loved hosting the sessions with the SAFFE Officer because he had a great passion for making a difference in our community. He was also a very motivational speaker. He knew how to engage the audience and give them a heartfelt call to action.

Learn To Dismiss The Naysayers

I had a lot of people who criticized my efforts. I had people say I was stupid for doing this type of thing. They said that things would never change. What they did not realize was that my efforts paid off with providing me with a safe and drug free environment where I would not have people steal my belongings. I also knew there had always been a clear disconnect between law enforcement and the general public and this was an opportunity to foster better relations.

I worked with our San Antonio Police Department's West Substation SAFFE Officers to create activities that nurtured positive relations between law enforcement and the community. I started with having a National Night Out at our home. I had a really good turn out the two years that I hosted the event. My neighbors were grateful that I had hosted it. We had a movie on the lawn event as part of our first National Night Out. It was a great success.

Our second year of National Night Out had a harvest theme. I hired Allan Hendrickson who is an awesome country music artist. He provided a live performance where he played his guitar and sang as we enjoyed our dinner. We had brisket, sausage, potato salad, corn on the cob, bread, and all the fixings. I had tea, lemonade, and soft drinks for beverages. I was proud to have our State Representative Justin Rodriguez and some of his staff in attendance at the event. I also had City Councilwoman Ana Sandoval send her staff with goodies to give away. They gave away table top recycle bins for organic foods.

I had a Movie on the Lawn for Halloween. It was a Disney cartoon movie called Hotel Transylvania. My brother and I made the screen that we used for the projector. I served hotdogs with all the fixings, popcorn, canned soft drinks, and Halloween buckets with full sized candies: Kit Kat, Snickers, M&Ms, and Almond Joy. It was a great opportunity to meet and greet others while enjoying a safe family activity. The event was a great success as we had a perfect turn out. We used up all of the chairs we had and then even laid out sleeping bags on the ground for the kids to lay down as they enjoyed the movie. The people even helped clean up after the event was over. It was such a big help too.

The school year was coming to an end and my neighbor Joseph Vasquez and I were concerned about the kids engaging in high risk behaviors. I decided to host a Drug Free Session at my home with an SAPD SAFFE Officer named Nathan Rodriguez. We did it the week before school let out for the Summer Break. We gave away Tee Shirts that said "Project 365…Making History" on them because we wanted to see evidence that positive change was occurring over the course of the year. We served pizza, popcorn, chips, and soft drinks. I had the opportunity to host Epi Quiorga at the event. He presented his NO BULLYING campaign. His presentation evoked a great deal of emotion because he spoke about his brother, Robert Quiroga, who was a professional boxer that had been murdered. He used his own testimony to emphasize how important it is to report bullying. He talked about how evil envy, jealousy, and rage can be. The participants took an oath promising to report dangerous behavior.

SAFFE Officer Nathan Rodriguez went over several different narcotics and what it was that parents could look for as signs of drug use and experimentation. I loved the way he connected with the community. He also had a passion for making a real difference. He had a great deal of empathy and compassion for others. He worked hard to help us as much as possible. When he promoted to detective, and became part of the Intelligence Unit, we were sad to see him go. We were happy that he had been promoted, but we knew the next guy would have big shoes to fill.

The latest event was at an apartment complex that is located very close to my home. There had been a lot of reports of shots fired and people had been shot several times at this complex. They were on the news frequently. SAFFE Officer, Eloy Medina, who had taken SAFFE Officer Nathan Rodriguez's position, helped me host a Basketball Shootout during Spring Break of 2020. The

SAFFE Officer brought the Corp program (formerly known as the Explorers) to the Basketball Shootout. I had tee shirts made that said, "Shoot Hoops Not Guns" on the back of the tee shirt with a picture of a basketball and hoop just above the words. The front of the tee shirt had the words "Spring Break 2020 Basketball Shoot Out" the bottom right had the words "SAPD West SAFFE unit."

I desperately wanted to create a bond between law enforcement and the general public. I served canned lemonade and tea, three types of flavored popcorn, and various flavored popsicles. I had two deputies from the Bexar County Constable's Office Precinct 2 in attendance as well. I had previously collaborated with them to host a Trunk or Treat event for Halloween at Precinct 2. We gave away popcorn and lemonade as well as candy bags with Halloween pencils, plastic spider rings, and candies. Constable Vasquez allowed the two deputies to attend the event and show their support. I was very grateful for their attendance. Their presence meant a lot to me.

SAPD Field Training Officer Carlos Sanchez impressed me. When I met this officer, I was intimidated by him. He had such a tough exterior, but I would later learn that he had such a different side to him. He has a huge heart. He took the time to listen to my concerns and offer advice and guidance. He helped me see things from a different perspective too. He encourages me and he helps me to stay motivated in my efforts to make a difference. He thanked me for what I did to help the neighborhood. He was a local who lived close by and made it known. He would also tell me not to let people get to me. He suggested I watch videos on YouTtube by Les Brown who is a prominent motivational speaker. I was immediately hooked. The videos not only inspired me, but gave me courage and the determination to keep moving forward. Officer Sanchez said not to worry about what people thought of me. He said that what was important was what I thought about myself. He showed he cared. This officer's actions helped me to rekindle the flame of determination and perseverance. We all need people like him in our lives. People are quick to forget the words you say, but they never forget how you made them feel. He gave me a feeling of affirmation and affiliation both at the same time. That meant a lot to me.

Unsung Heroes

I have to give special recognition to these four officers: Elliott Valdez, Nathan Rodriguez, Eloy Medina, and Carlos Sanchez because they gave me an opportunity to try and make a significant difference in my community. Their experience and expertise was evident in the way that they interacted with the public. They all want what is best for the community and it comes across with such profound passion. There is good and bad in every organization. Negative attention is so easily found, yet positive attention is so easily dismissed. People love to be affirmed for the work that they do. Unfortunately, our vested efforts were not publicized in the newspaper or on the evening news. None of us thought to call the media because we were not in it for the public attention. Unsung heroes remain unrecognized and it is such a shame. I want these men to know they matter and that we care. I appreciate all that they do to make a difference in our communities and I want there to be more efforts at community policing. It needs to be a vested effort on all parts if we are to make a real difference.

I know that growing up in the neighborhood I never had a National Night Out event that I ever went too. I sure did not attend any basketball shoot outs or Drug Free sessions, or Movies On The Lawn either. I wanted to take all the nurturing I was able to get growing up and pay it forward in my own authentic way. I never sought any recognition or notoriety either. I had no need for the spotlight. My satisfaction came from seeing a positive difference. That was my payback.

I realize that some people want the fame and to be in the spotlight and they do things for the wrong reasons. I am not seeking affirmation from others. I truly want to serve in ways that cause me to feel soulfulness and peace in my heart. People can eventually see the difference.

I was raised to be humble. We were told never to show off because it was in poor taste. I know who I am and what I am all about. God sees all. I try to pay it forward as much as I can. I try to acknowledge those who do more than what is expected. I cherish those who look out for me and try and be there for me when I need someone to talk to or to help me in anyway.

It seems that people now- a-days want to portray such an image of sophistication, of glamour, or of intellect. Too bad that people buy into all of that and don't get to know these people for whom they really are. It always amazed me how people who look the part get the part. Those of us who stay humble simply get passed up. It happens time and time again.

Your Generosity Will Make A Difference

Giving back and paying it forward is important. It is not about trying to be in the spotlight, but about trying to leave this place a little better than how we found it. Don't forget to bless others in ways that make a real difference. It makes things much better for everyone. God knows your heart. He knows your intent, and he blesses those who give unconditionally. I urge you to try and pay it forward every chance you get. You truly reap what you sow.

Take the opportunity to create change. It can be as simple as sharing your story with someone else. It can encourage those who are trying to get to the next level. It does not have to be about money. It can be volunteering your time and your energy. It only has to come from the heart, be genuine, and to be a selfless act done to improve, inspire, or motivate others. The next chapter will be about planting seeds.

Chapter Summary/Key Takeaways

- Follow YOUR passion even if others do not agree with it.

- Give back to your community in some way and do it for the right reason.

- Don't do it because you want to be famous and get the recognition

- Do it because you care to bring about some type of positive change.

- Write down three ways you can pay it forward.

- Who can help you to be part of the positive change?

- How can you get others to become actively involved?

CHAPTER SIX

Planting Seeds

We should continuously plant seeds of hope. Each person has their unique circumstances and their own way of working through them. Even when we think they are not listening, they are. My Mary Kay Director, Muriel Perez, would tell me "When you are sharing the opportunity with people remember some are like toasters and pop right up and do the work while others are like crock pots and they slowly marinate and then get the work done." I find that people are that way with a lot of other things too. There are people who learn from watching and others that learn by doing. Everyone is different. What I do know for sure is that they are watching and listening to everything that goes on. They are constantly making connections about the world around them.

When they are finally ready to move forward, they will remember the information and the advice you gave them. Certain conditions have to be met before they can take action, and those conditions are specific to each and every one of us. When the Aha moment happens, and they are ready, those seeds will sprout. Not only will they sprout but those roots will be long and deep. The roots symbolize our commitment and our dedication. To be deeply rooted means that our passion is greater than the obstacles that stand in the way. Roots have a lot to do with our "Why?" Our why has a lot to do with the passion and the commitment involved.

We Are All At Different Stages

Everyone is at a different place in life. Their situations vary. Some people have to fertilize their soil. Others need more water, and still others need more sunshine. Fertilizer helps things grow. That can be positive comments and encouragement. It can be opportunities for growth. It can even be just a rewiring of our thinking so that we can evolve.

The way we process information is important. I tend to want to overanalyze things, but I see the importance of looking at things in the physical realm and in the spiritual realm as well. There needs to be a great balance of rationale and spiritual guidance. I do as much as I can and I leave the rest to God in prayerful petitions.

When I taught in the public schools I loved to have students create interactive notebooks. I had them use the black and white composition books that you can buy at the dollar store. They could add comments and draw or write in them so that they were physically showing the connections they were making between the content being presented and the world around them. I would create what I call chicken strips. They were given information on a long strip of paper. We would go over the content then they would add their own connections about this information and relate it to something else.

They would include mind maps and other graphic organizers that helped them to organize the information. These actions helped with memory, recall, and helped the students reach those higher order thinking skills of application, evaluation, synthesis, analysis and so forth. They could review their information and were able to use their visuals to take the deep dive into the learning process.

Life requires a detailed mind map. The mind map grows over time. It is malleable. The more detailed the mind map the deeper the dive taken in the learning process. When we plant seeds of hope, and those seeds sprout, neuro-connections grow. They expand their knowledge, their understanding of what is possible, and they expand their faith in the world and in themselves. I strive to create life-long learners out of my students. We are all constantly evolving. We should never stay stagnant.

Planting seeds can mean that we simply suggest something to someone or share an opportunity. It can be exposing them to things they didn't know about before. It can be sharing information that you think my improve a situation or circumstance and allowing the idea to settle in and in the meantime use that methodology. Let people see you model the idea and let them see the results. So many times, people want to see other people try things before they venture to try and make it happen for them.

The social-emotional part of each of us bears scars and hesitates to make ourselves vulnerable again for fear of being hurt. We put our guard up or close ourselves off as a defense for fear of being attacked. What we do not realize is that we are closing the doors to opportunity when we do that. We are not balancing the natural with the supernatural.

Walk by Faith

Step out in faith and leave the rest to God. I am almost 50 and I had never felt the love and care I am just now feeling from a man who I feel deserves me. I wanted someone that would show me they cared with their actions and not their words. For years I prayed that God would allow someone with good intentions to come into my life, and for years I remained alone. It wasn't until I learned to heal my wounds that I was able to move forward and quit looking back at the past. It took courage and it took faith to get me to try again. I had already given up on the idea that I would find someone to truly love me and care for me the way I felt I deserved to be loved and cared for. I did not want someone who thought I was convenient, but that I was whole heartedly worthy of their love and affection.

I feel like the constant prayer and the holding off to find what I really wanted finally paid off. I planted the seed by praying in detail. I asked God to bring me a man that would be affectionate and kind. A man that would show me he loved me in his actions and not just his words. I wanted a man who was family oriented and who loved children. I wanted someone that had a great work ethic and that would understand that I also needed my freedom to grow personally and professionally. The idea of being equally yoked was important to me. I wanted to share the same beliefs and the same goals. I watered those seeds daily by constantly being in prayer and meditation about what that kind of relationship would look like, what it would feel like, and how it might sound when we spoke to each other.

I am glad I never gave up on finding love and I am glad that God stepped in and made it happen. He used those closest to me to nurture the relationship into existence and I am forever grateful. I joked with them that I wanted a warranty or return policy but there was no need the relationship flourished when I prayed to God asking him for what I wanted in my future husband. I would later learn that I needed to let go and let God. I would learn that planting seeds works in the physical realm and in the spiritual realm as well.

One of the biggest concepts that I learned about planting seeds is to check the ground where I plant them. If its rocky soil, I need to find more fertile ground. If a person is bitter, angry and just not open to receiving, we may need to come back at a later date. We can expose them to the information or suggestion and let it marinate. Don't do anything else but encourage them. When they are ready, they will seek you out to help them deal with that situation. The ground can change once we remove the rocks it becomes much more fertile.

I encourage all of you to step out in faith and plant seeds. Many times we do not speak up because we feel that the information or suggestion may not be well received. I promise you that they hear you. They just need more time before they truly listen. My desire is for people to continue to motivate, inspire, and encourage others. Seeds only sprout when they are planted, buried in the ground, watered, fertilized and placed in the sun. The next chapter will be about finding bliss in an uncertain time.

Chapter Summary/Key Takeaways

- We must all learn to plant seeds by sharing information and suggestions to people.

- Remember that everyone is at a different place in life.

- Certain conditions must be met before people can move forward and seek advancement.

- Everyone deserves to have people share opportunities with them.

- How can you inspire someone to advance or stretch their learning outside of their comfort zone?

- Set aside time to share information with people in a meaningful way

CHAPTER SEVEN

Finding Bliss in Uncertain Times

Bliss is defined as perfect happiness and great joy. Bliss comes from the knowledge that what you have and who you have around you is in it for the long haul and that they have your best interests in mind. Bliss is not about having an abundance of material luxuries but more about being grounded and stable. God gives us discernment and lets us make sense of the world by determining whether the fruits of the spirit are in place or not. We should all try and demonstrate these fruits of the spirit and not worry so much about things that are temporal.

Living In Gratitude

Internal strength, solitude, and self-awareness breeds confidence in yourself and in those you have around you. Happiness can come from comfort and peace. Let your bliss revolve around the gratitude you have for what God has provided you. The mere fact that no matter where you are God is with you should bring you happiness. We need not give value to things that are temporal. Material things come and go, but spiritual wealth remains. Love is priceless! Unity among loved ones brings feelings of security and safety.

Possessions and Position DO NOT Define You

Do not allow yourself to be evaluated by the type of car you drive, the size of your house, your career, or your bank account. These things can make people puffed up and proud. God wants us to take pride in our righteous living and our service to others. Be proud to serve a heavenly father who shows us an unconditional love. Value yourself for the righteous living that you demonstrate. Value yourself for the positive relationship and constant dialog you have with your heavenly father. Let those things measure your development and your personal increase in wisdom and patience.

All That Glitters Is Not Gold

All that glitters is not gold! People tend to portray an image of sophistication and riches, but that is not bliss. Bliss comes from hard work, dedication, righteous living and servant leadership. Sometimes, what we see on the outside is not the person's true sense of self. I know people who seem to have it all together because of their wealth and material possessions, but inside they are dying for lack of true love and real affection. I would rather be materially poor and be spiritually rich. I see people who truly depend on the Lord for their day to needs to be met and they are some of the happiest people I know. I think it is because they truly understand what it is like to depend completely on their higher power and to see the manifestation of those things they most needed at just the right timing does something to create a deep and meaningful testimony that people can't compare with anything else.

Your relationship with your higher power should come first! Once that relationship is established and strong, everything else falls into place. God wants us to rely on him. He wants us to live life more abundantly. God wants us to be good stewards in all of our ways. Do we handle our finances well? Do we handle our relationships well? Are we serving others the way he wants us to? When we live life according to his will his blessings will be bestowed upon us.

Bliss comes from the grace God offers and not as a reward of the good deeds we do. Bliss is being in God's presence and knowing you are in congruence with his will. There is a peace and a favor that you find when you submit yourself completely to Christ. It is only then that we can truly experience the idea of bliss in our lifetime. Some people have a misconception of what bliss requires and what you have to do to have it manifest in your life.

I find happiness in the simplest of things. I love spending time with people I care for. Just spending time with them in meaningful ways makes me happy. I love cooking in the kitchen with my boyfriend. I love listening to great music and enjoying a meal as we listen to it. I love having time holding one another and feeling fulfilled because the touching shows affection and care.

Don't make bliss about luxurious items and temporal things that do not matter. Look out for one another. Be of service to those you love. Keep communication flowing and be brutally honest with one another so that there are no surprises and you are on the same page. Stay in gratitude for the things that God has provided to you.

Chapter Summary/Key Takeaways

- Finding Bliss is not about material possessions and temporal things.

- Be in constant gratitude for what God has provided you.

- Bliss comes from the knowledge that what you have and who you have around you is in it for the long haul and that they have your best interests in mind.

- Take time to write down the many blessings that you thank God for.

CHAPTER EIGHT

Forgiveness Allows Development

So many times I see people get stuck in their own emotions and perceptions of the world. A traumatic event can cause you to see the world in a different way. It changes your perspective and often times it takes a lot to get past that feeling of being stuck. It reminds me of a callous. When you have a callous you have less feeling in that area and the feeling of the callous itself is rather rough and hard. I think our hearts are much the same way. It is when we can forgive ourselves and the people around us that we can develop in much more meaningful ways.

Wash Yourself Clean

When we forgive people for wrong doings, or we forgive ourselves for things we think we did wrong, we allow Jesus to wash us clean. We need to invite the spirit of Jesus to join us in washing away all the pain and mistakes from your past. The Lord's love is so great that he washed the feet of his apostles. He loved them so much that he assumed the role of the lowest servant and washed the disciple's feet after they had been walking around the dirty streets of Jerusalem. There was a need to cleanse them to demonstrate an action that showed his love for them.

Holding on to anger, grief, and anxiety wears us out because it depletes us of our energy and does not allow the Holy Spirit to dwell in us. You cannot attract love and happiness when you are filled with negativity. It is like a magnet turned the other way around. It either attracts or repels. Let your forgiveness bring you a sense of peace. Let the idea that you forgive settle deep in your soul. Forgiveness is for you not for the other party. You can end a relationship and still be able to forgive them for their wrongdoings.

Mature In This Earthly Life

Our ability to forgive is essential if we are to mature in our Earthy life. There will always be people who don't see things our way. There will always be people who disagree with us about how we live or how we think. Our way of life or ideals may anger them, but it is ok to agree to disagree. The world would be a much better place if we learned to understand before seeking to be understood. We tend to want things to be the way we want them to be, but the truth is that every person has a different set of morals and beliefs. We should celebrate diversity and not be so rigid about wanting people to be just like us.

I know I have grown a great deal in this aspect. I tend to be a very serious person. I get my feelings hurt quiet easily sometimes and I wear my heart on my sleeve so to speak, but I have learned to build walls and use them when necessary. The idea is not to stay stuck in a bad relationship because no one wants that, rather to leave the relationship and be able to move on with life by forgiving ourselves and our partner for the fact that we weren't able to make it a successful healthy relationship. Wash yourself clean in God's abiding love and move forward with peace and tranquility knowing God had more in store and that this was not it. He will never ask you to give up something unless he has something greater in store for you. I have seen it happen to me and I know he will do it for you too.

Have Faith In God's Promises

Have unwavering faith in God's promises and know that no matter what happens God is with you in spirit and that all you have to do is talk to him. Pray to him for guidance and for clarity. Ask him to give you peace and tranquility as you move forward in your life and leave the past behind you. You can't drive looking in the rearview mirror. That is why windshields are so big and rear view mirrors are so small. We were meant to look forward and occasionally glance back when necessary. Our past does teach us many lessons. There is no doubt. The next chapter is about cleaning house

Chapter Summary/Key Takeaways

- Forgiveness brings you peace and tranquility

- We must allow forgiveness to exist before we can attract the Holy Spirit

- Unforgiveness brings anxiety, grief, and depression

- When we forgive we are cleansing ourselves in God's holy spirit

- Write down a list of people you need to forgive. Write down what you are forgiveing them for and in detail how it made you feel and end the list with the words "I no longer carry this burden of grief and unhappiness. I bring it to the cross for you to deal with Lord. May your will be done. I declare and decree my soul and spirit cleansed by the blood of Jesus of any anger, frustration, and strife in the name of Jesus Christ Amen."

CHAPTER NINE

Walk In Your Own Authority

We do not need to have a title or a degree to get out and do what we were meant to do in life. I know each of us has God given gifts that he wants us to exercise and share. Many of us have callings that we feel we should be doing but we have that unworthy feeling thinking we are not equipped for that part. God equips those that are called he does not call those who are equipped. He loves us all and gave us all unique gifts. Take your gift and run with it. Allow yourself to venture beyond your comfort zone and experience new techniques and strategies to grow that gift and allow it to prosper. Your success comes from serving God and living righteously.

Honor God

When we use our God given gifts, we honor God. He wants us to use these gifts and allow them to bear fruit. I know I had a calling for years before I had the courage and confidence to share my story and exercise my unrefined gift with the world. I am surrounding myself with positive people who are willing to be a solid foundation that I can build from. I am learning new things all the time. Life-long learning is essential because we live in a dynamic world. It is always changing.

Lean On Your Higher Power

Allow yourself to lean on your higher power when you feel defeated and you lack energy and motivation. People will fail you because they are imperfect beings but God is the same yesterday, today, and tomorrow. Rely on him and make him your center and he will allow you to walk in confidence in your own God given authority. When you put God first in your life everything else eventually falls right into place. Lean on that higher power to see you through.

Find what it is that you love doing and that you do with the least amount of effort. That just may be the gift God gave you. Explore these options with fervor because God wants us to live life more abundantly. He wants you to find that gift and pray to him to guide you to the right network of people. When God predestines for things to happen there is nothing that can stand in our way.

Walk in Authority

I learned to walk in my own authority. I tell myself I am a daughter of the King of Kings and because I love him and try to live my life righteously he will not leave me. I am unstoppable and obstacles that lie before me will be overcome. The word of God will not come back void. I will therefore step out in my God given authority to seek to be a catalyst of hope and or positive change. I know I will encounter opposition and I will lean on my higher power to see me through. I long to reach out to a multitude of people as God works through me to help them improve their quality of life and feel more joy, confidence and success. Claim your own authority with sincerity and say it with conviction. What you put out into the universe has a corresponding reaction.

I challenge you to step out in faith and go after your biggest dreams! Go all in and give it your 100%. God's promises do not come back null and void they grow a deeper testimony. Our faith grows with each new development and advancement. The combination of time, effort and consistency will eventually pay off and you will know it was your God who brought you through it all. Walk with your head held high knowing that the mental strength and aptitude you hold comes from your heavenly Father.

I would encourage you to do some goal setting and map out a roadmap on how to reach your destination. Believe you CAN reach this destination and have faith in God and yourself. Do not give up. Research and find people who are doing what you want to do and reach out to these people for advice and counsel. There are many people who know God was in the midst of their struggle and they give back by paying it forward. I would advise you to speak from the heart and not try to be anything but your authentic self. The success will come when preparation meets opportunity. Open your heart and your mind and know you are worthy to receive. Our next chapter is about telling you that your best is yet to come.

Chapter Summary/Key Takeaways

- Believe in yourself and know God is in control.

- Walk in the authority God gives you.

- Know there are people to mentor and guide you wholeheartedly.

- Do not give up and know that the struggle allows us to build a testimony

- Make a list of the things you think may be your God given gifts.

- Write steps you can take to grow these gifts and refine them in a way that serves others.

CHAPTER TEN

Your Best Is Yet To Come

Your best is yet to come! Know that all you have to do is step out in your God given authority and go all in! God is waiting on you and so are the people who will benefit from your gift. Do not waste any more time. You were meant for so much more than what you have now. Take that leap of faith and hit the ground running. Gain momentum and stay in motion. Your best awaits you. Remember to disregard the naysayers. Believe in yourself. Know that your struggle will end when you are ready to submit totally to your higher power and make that your focus. Everything will start to fall into place. You will start to see increase in your life. Your spirit will be at peace and content to know that you took the leap of faith and are succeeding. I know that people say that the way to Jesus is a long and narrow path. Remember the analogy of the cocoon. Sometimes it is ok to be alone or in a smaller circle as you evolve. Know that your gift can mean big differences in your life and remember to pay it forward.

It Is Never Too Late

It is never too late to set a goal and go after it. Stay in prayer. Surround yourself with people who add to you and who do not deplete you of energy and resources. Life is short and we have to make the most of it. The hardest part is the beginning. Once you get started and you build momentum the rest comes faster than you think it will. Allow yourself to be coachable. New strategies and new techniques will allow you get to your destination faster. Remember to be in gratitude for all that you learn and all that God gives you. God will bring you new people to allow you to grow. He will give you resources you thought were never possible. He has been waiting for you to trust in him. He is standing there with open arms saying, "My child I am here for you just step out in faith!" Do not live with the regret of never having tried. The world is out there for you to partake of it. You just have to go out there and get what is meant to be yours.

There Is No Health Without Mental Health

I care about people learning that they can do anything they set out to do. I care about the mental health of those in my community and elsewhere. There is no health without mental health. It all starts with our thoughts. Think that you have all you need right now right there inside you. You are worthy of greatness, of love, and of earning large amounts of money. Our mindset has everything to do with our success. Our success comes from serving God. One touch of God's favor is greater than a lifetime of labor. Stay humble and know that God touches those who serve him and live righteously.

Chapter Summary/Key Takeaways

- Believe you have everything you need within you right now to be successful

- God will uplift you and give you favor

- You are worthy and unstoppable

- It is never too late to begin to reach your goal of refining your God Given Gifts

- Your best is yet to come!

- Write down God's promises that support the idea that he wants more for you and that he will support you through the process.

- Place these writings in prominent places where you will see them frequently

- Spend time in prayer asking God for what you want to accomplish using detailed imagery

EPILOGUE / CONCLUSION

Being resilient, having tenacity, and overcoming adversity all require that you really get to know who you are at your very core. They require you to reexamine how you deal with problem situations, and how you pour back into yourself so that you are in alignment with the universe. Stay focused on your goals and aspirations. Make sure your behaviors and actions are congruent with what you are trying to accomplish. Create a safety net of people who can and will inspire, and support you in your efforts. Remember that as we grow we need to change our programming. Replace bad habits with good ones. This will help you to evolve into a better sense of yourself.

BIBLIOGRAPHY

Meichenbaum, D. (2011). Resiliency Building as a means to prevent PTSD and related adjustment problems in military personnel. In B.A. Moore and W.F. Penk (Eds.). <u>Treating PTSD in military personnel: A Clinical Handbook.</u> New York: Guilford Press

ACKNOWLEDGMENTS

I want to thank my family for believing in me. I know I sometimes come across as crazy. I am crazy. I am crazy about you. I want to give you the very best that I can. I know I don't often acknowledge you the way that I should. I want you to know I am so proud of you. Marcelina and Raul, you two have a heart of gold and your actions and behaviors inspired me to write this book. We all have things we struggle with and obstacles that come about, but you two help me to work past all of that. I love you both very much.

Mom, thank you for encouraging me and challenging me to do more. Dad, I know you are with me in spirit and I know you are advocating for me on the other side. Thank you for all your lessons. Thank you for all the values and morals you taught me and for teaching me to value myself so that others will value me too.

I want to thank Daniel Gomez and Mari Gomez for allowing me to understand my worth. Thank you for inspiring me to do more with my life too. I also want to thank Michael D. Butler and his publishing company, Beyond Publishing, for helping me bring the idea of writing a book to fruition. This is a dream come true. It means a lot and I will be forever grateful.

ABOUT THE AUTHOR

Elizabeth Ann Maldonado is a Certified Teacher, Certified Life Coach, Ordained Minister, and Motivational Speaker. She earned her Bachelor of Arts degree in Interdisciplinary Studies with a concentration in Generic Special Education from The University of the Incarnate Word. She graduated with honors: Cum Laude. She is a San Antonio, Texas native. She graduated from Oliver Wendell Holmes High School which is on the west side of San Antonio, Texas where she still resides.

Her passion has always been working with at risk youth. She created her own educational homeschooling program called Innovative Approaches to Education. www.ia2ed.com and she later created Elizabeth's Life Coaching as a continuum of services for the people who needed a more one to one approach to break through plateaus and overcome obstacles.

She has served as a special education teacher for over twenty years. She is very active in her community and enjoys working collaboratively with other entities to improve people's quality of life. She is single and has no children at this time. She enjoys spending quality time with family and friends and she enjoys cooking, listening to music, and being at one with nature.